PRESENTED BY

GTE SOUTH DAKOTA
630 2nd Street

DR. CURTIS R. JOHNSON
610 Main Street
583-4310

FARMERS & MERCHANTS STATE BANK
550 Main Street
583-2234

Ray Diede
SCOTLAND REDI-MIX
420 Railway
583-4301

Greg & JoAnn Gemar
GEMAR'S MARKET
510 2nd Street
583-2236

SCOTLAND, SOUTH DAKOTA

Coordinated by Master Marketing Corporation, Hawarden, Iowa

Don't Take Candy From A Stranger

A Parents' Record & Child Protection Guide

Started On:

_____

Prepared By

_____

For

Designed and Developed
by
Oleg Kay

Edited by Vivian Carpenter

Bayberry Books

All rights reserved under International and Pan American Copyright Conventions.
Published in the United States by Bayberry Books,
a division of Stampley Enterprises, Inc., Charlotte, NC 28233.

ISBN — 0-915741-01-6

Manufactured in the United States of America

Note to Parents

Child disappearance has become a national tragedy. Runaways, abductions, crime, divorce and various other circumstances have created grim statistics. Without warning or cause, it can happen to any family. On the average of once each minute, a child vanishes from a schoolyard, shopping mall, supermarket or even his own home. Every child is vulnerable. It is imperative that young children be taught the rules of safety and self-protection.

An informed child is a safer child. Unfortunately, too many parents are caught off guard.

Many a missing child would be safely at home today if his parents had openly discussed with him the facts of abduction. There is less likelihood that a child will be victimized if he hears in plain words about molestation, sexual abuse.

Your child needs to know the difference between a friend and an acquaintance. A stranger is a person who is NOT a friend. Acquaintances are strangers. It is usually an acquaintance who molests or abducts a child. Children are friendly, outgoing and obedient. They must be taught caution; to say NO to an adult in a frightening or uncomfortable situation.

Adult responsibility demands that children be taught the skills of safety and self-protection. Deliver your child from most threatening circumstances and give yourself peace of mind — BE INFORMED!

Fingerprinting: Recently, local Parent-Teacher Associations, schools, state and local police, churches, businesses and civic groups have initiated programs to fingerprint children. It is voluntary, with parental permission. The parent keeps the only record. Fingerprinting aids law enforcement agencies in an emergency if a child is lost, has run away or is abducted.

Record Keeping: The National Child Safety Council recommends keeping up-to-date records on each child: a good color photograph (current each year), a medical and dental history, a physical description including height, weight, color of eyes and hair. Any scar, birthmark or other distinguishing characteristic should be noted.

This publication proposes to help make your child abduction-proof and to provide one convenient place for a fingerprint card, pictorial record and your child's vital statistics.

Hopefully, you will never need to use these records.

THE WORST THING YOU CAN DO IS NOTHING.

Child Lures

Enticing a child in order to take advantage of him is routine procedure for child molesters. The oldest and most common lure is to offer the child candy, toys or gifts in exchange for favors.

Other frequent lures are: to ask a child to help find a lost pet, to ask directions to a nearby school or park, to ask help in carrying packages to a door or a car. Abductors have been known to disguise themselves as elderly or disabled people.

Children are easily lured when called by name. A child's name often appears on his T-shirt, lunch box or bicycle plate.

Quite often children are lured into fun games where intimate body contact is used.

Children are often lured by secret promises of modeling jobs, photo sessions and other opportunities to make a lot of money. The child is usually told to keep it secret from his parents. These situations quite often result in seductions and child pornography.

Child abductors use stories to confuse and worry a child by telling him his mother is ill or was taken to a hospital or that his father was in an accident or that his house is on fire, etc., with the view of getting the child to accompany them.

Other abductors will use abusive and threatening language to frighten a child into submission.

It is sad but true that most child abductors and molesters and murderers are adults with whom the child is acquainted. Sometimes it is a family member, neightbor, etc.

Be alert! Be on guard for adults who show unusual interest in your child. If you see your child with candy, money, a new toy or other unfamiliar items that did not come from you, question your child in a subtle manner. Beware of fun and games between your child and an adult where much body contact is used. If you learn that your child has been or is going to a job interview (i.e. baby-sitting, etc.) find out subtly when, where and for whom. It is important that your child knows you love him. Keep all lines of communication between you and your child open.

On the following page are basic rules for your child's self-protection.

Teaching Your Child Self-Protection
Some "Do's and Don'ts"

1. Children should avoid all strangers.

2. Teach your child to scream "HELP" when in a frightening situation.

3. Make certain your child knows his full name, address, city, state and telephone number.

4. Tell your child that policemen are his friends, especially when he is lost or frightened.

5. Instruct your child that he is never to go near a car if a stranger calls him.

6. Teach your child that he is not to be fooled by a stranger because he knows his name.

7. Never accept a ride from a stranger, regardless of weather conditions.

8. Never take candy, a beverage, food or anything else from a stranger.

9. Tell your child never to hide in a deserted place in order to escape from a stranger.

10. Tell your child never to go into an empty house.

11. Instruct your child never to take isolated short cuts to or from school, playgrounds or local stores.

12. Teach your child that no one has the right to touch him or ask him to keep a secret from you.

13. Teach your child to notify you immediately of any strangers loitering near school, playground or in the neighborhood.

14. Teach your child that a stranger can be someone whom he sees pass by often but does not really know.

15. Teach your child to walk or run in the opposite direction if he thinks a car or van is following him.

16. If your child suspects he is being followed by someone on foot, instruct him to run; yell "HELP"; attract the attention of another person; run to the nearest public place or store and tell those inside what is happening.

17. Your child must be taught that adults do not need a child's help to find a lost pet or show them directions. Adults should always ask other adults for help.

18. Assure your child that if he gets lost or is taken out of town and needs help to dial "0" from the nearest phone and ask for the Police.

Rules For Child Protection

1. *Young children should be under adult supervision at all times.*

2. *Never leave your child alone in a car, at home, in a public bathroom, supermarket, in a parking lot or shopping center.*

3. *When shopping, show your child where the courtesy desk is or simply instruct him to go to the nearest checkout counter and ask for help, if you and he become separated.*

4. *Photographs should be taken at least once a year of children past five years of age; two times a year for a child between the ages of two and five and four times a year when the child is under two.*

5. *Keep an up-to-date record of your child's medical and dental history and photographs with a detailed description.*

6. *Make certain your child knows you love him.*

7. *Your child must know his full name, address, city and state in which he lives.*

8. *Teach your child to scream for "HELP" in what he feels is a frightening situation.*

9. *Should a stranger do something scary to your child, notify police immediately.*

10. *Make a game of practicing to describe strangers with your child. Was he tall or short; fat or thin; had he light or dark hair; have a beard or clean shaven; wear a tie or eye glasses? What color were his shoes or shirt? Then, if your child should ever be approached by a stranger, he will know exactly how to describe him to you and the police.*

11. *If you ever plan to have your child picked up by a friend, make up a "secret code word" for you and your child that the friend must use.*

12. *If your child must be absent from school — call the school. If your child does not show up at school, arrange to have the school call you.*

13. *Have your child practice using a real telephone. Let him do the dialing when calling grandmother, aunt, uncle or dad at work. Explain what an area code is and what it does. There is no substitute for experience.*

14. *Do not buy T-shirts, lunch boxes or bicycle personalized with your child's name. Children respond to strangers when called by name.*

15. *When your child goes to the candy store, park or playground, have him "buddy-up" because there is security in numbers.*

16. *If your child is ever home alone, instruct him to never answer the door or tell anyone on the phone that he is alone. Leave your child a telephone number where he can reach you. Have him check in with a neighbor, he will feel better and so will you.*

17. *When you are not around, make certain your child is playing with other children whose parents are aware of your absence.*

8. When driving with your child, play the game of identifying license plates from other states.

9. In the event of separation or divorce, make certain your child's nursery, school, camp and baby sitter do not release your child to anyone who is not authorized by you.

0. The most important thing your child must know is his full name, address and how to dial "0" to call the Police.

1. Be alert! If you discover your child with a new toy, money, candy or any other item that did not come from you, discover the source.

Notes To Separated or Divorced Parents

If you have legal custody and there is friction between you and your former spouse, take the following precautions:

1. Have a copy of your child's birth certificate.

2. Obtain a Social Security card for your child.

3. Obtain a passport for your child. Instruct the Passport Office that your child can leave the country only with the consent of both parents.

4. Keep a file containing your former spouse's Social Security, credit card and driver's license numbers together with a description of his or her automobile. Also keep a list of his/her friends and relatives.

5. Try to stay on friendly terms with your former spouse and in-laws.

6. Engrave his Social Security number on any article your child uses constantly such as a lunch box, eye glasses, etc.

7. Keep all medical records current with dates, names, addresses and phone numbers of doctors and hospitals having your child's records.

8. His dental records are as unique as your child's fingerprints. Make certain the dentist maintains up-to-date and complete records.

9. It is of the utmost importance that your child is assured of your love for him and that he has the right to find you regardless of what anyone else tells him.

10. In the event of a serious conflict over the child with an estranged spouse, your first consideration is to obtain permanent or temporary legal custody. Without it you have no legal recourse if your spouse abducts the child.

11. If you have suspicions about a possible abduction of your child by your former spouse, request the Court for a large bond to be posted to guarantee his visitation rights.

Emergency Steps
In the event your child is lost

1. *Check your house thoroughly; contact your neighbors and all nearby friends and relatives. Exhaust all reasonable possibilities. Only then, call the police.*

2. *Check your room and your child's room for clues or correspondence that might indicate a runaway.*

3. *Call the State Police.*

4. *Call the Sheriff's Office.*

5. *Call the FBI and demand that your report be entered into their National Crime Information Center (NCIC) computer.*

6.   *CHILD FIND, INC. HOT LINE   1-800-I AM LOST (1-800-426-5678)*

   Child Find, Inc. is a national non-profit organization dedicated to the well-being of children. It operates a 24-hour toll free number: 1-800-I AM LOST. Teach your children this number to if they are lost or need help. Be sure your child always carries enough change to make a phone call.

   — MISSING CHILD NATIONAL HOT LINE —
   1-800-843-5678

   Call toll-free 1-800-843-5678 "hot line" for Missing and Exploited Children. This is a federally funded national agency created to receive and dispatch critical leads from all callers. All information is gathered on computers and dispatched to your local state and federal law enforcement agencies.

7. *Call your local newspaper, television and radio stations.*

8. *Publicize your story with a photo of the missing child with a detailed description and your telephone number.*

9. *Contact your local government respresentatives.*

10. *Distribute posters of your child's photo and description far and wide along with contact telephone numbers.*

11. *Keep your telephone lines open.*

   WHEN YOUR CHILD IS FOUND, DO NOT FAIL TO NOTIFY EVERYONE IMMEDIATELY.

To prevent your child from becoming a statistic, teach him self-protection by discussing the dangers point-by-point.

THE WORST THING YOU CAN DO IS NOTHING.

Child Abuse

Ideally, a newborn child brings to his parents a sense of joy, of wonder. Ideally, that child is nurtured and grows physically, mentally, spiritually and emotionally toward the day of his own adulthood, perhaps parenthood. This is the life cycle as is intended.

The care and protection of a child is an enormous and rewarding experience. How heart breaking, how infuriating to think that an innocent child can become the object of molestation, of child abuse.

An epidemic number of people live today crippled emotionally, unable to live full and happy lives — victims of abuse.

Partly because of reluctance to face such a sickening fact, parents are ignorant of what is happening to their own child. Caught unaware, a parent reacts with disbelief and revulsion.

It may not be easy to talk to a child about molestation but it has become a necessity. It can happen to any child!

Child molesters are sick people. Sexually abused and molested children are most often the victims of people they know and trust — family members, neighbors, friends. One victim in five is less than seven years of age. Boys and infants are not exempt. Many child abusers were themselves abused as children.

Some indications to watch for:

(1) Rather sudden personality change.
(2) Outgoing child becomes withdrawn, insecure.
(3) Change in sleep, eating, toilet habits.
(4) Increase in behavior problems.
(5) Surprising interest in subject of sex, genitals.

To prevent sexual abuse:

(1) If you discover your child with a new toy, money, candy or any "favor" that did not come from you, find out the source.
(2) A child must know his rights. Tell your child that no adult may touch any part of him/her that is covered by a bathing suit.
(3) Assure your child of your love. Make sure he understands that his body is private. No one has the right to touch him or to ask him to keep a secret from you.
(4) Telling your child to say "no" is not enough. Sexual abuse can happen. Your child must be able to confide in you without losing your love.
(5) Be explicit! Confront the issue directly. Tell your child that no one, absolutely no one, *is to touch or fondle any private parts of his body.*
(6) Watch out for adults who manipulate children into fun games which result in intimate body contact.
(7) Believe in your child and listen to him. Communicate with openness.

If you need help, GET IT. There are now many competent agencies and experts in this field.

13

Attach
Hair
Sample

Place Photo Inside
This Frame

Date Photo Taken _____

Child's Full Name _____ *Nickname* _____

Age _____ *Weight* _____ *Height* _____ *Color: Eyes* _____ *Hair* _____

Right or Left Handed? _____ *Complexion* _____

Glasses? _____ *Contact Lenses?* _____

15

Personal Facts

Child's Full Name _____

Place of Birth: City_____ State _____

Location of Birth Certificate_____

Social Security No. _____

Current Address

Street_____ Date _____

City_____ State _____

Mother's Maiden Name _____

Place of Birth: City_____ State _____

Birth Date _____

Social Security Number MONTH   DAY   YEAR

_____

Father's Full Name _____

Place of Birth: City_____ State _____

Birth Date _____

Social Security Number MONTH   DAY   YEAR

Nearest Relatives — Names, Addresses & Telephone Numbers

Name _____ Relation _____ Telephone _____

Address _____

Name _____ Relation _____ Telephone _____

Address _____

Name _____ Relation _____ Telephone _____

Address _____

Name _____ Relation _____ Telephone _____

Address _____

Name _____ Relation _____ Telephone _____

Address _____

Personal Facts

Likes and Dislikes _____ Date _____

_____

_____

_____

Habits _____

_____

_____

_____

Close Friends _____

_____

_____

_____

Special (Influential) People _____

_____

_____

_____

Favorite Clothing _____

_____

Colors _____

_____

Favorite Pastime _____

_____

Transportation To and From School _____

_____

After School Activities (Around the Neighborhood) _____

_____

_____

Other _____

_____

_____

Immunizations Record

Child's Name _____

Doctor _____

Address _____ Telephone _____

	EXACT DATES		EXACT DATES BOOSTERS	
Smallpox Vaccination _____				
Diphtheria, Tetanus, Whooping Cough ____				
Polio _____				
Mumps _____				
Rubella _____				
Measles _____				
Other _____				

Previous Health History

(Check the following diseases which your child has had)

Rheumatic Fever ☐   Poliomyelitis ☐   Scarlet Fever ☐

Chickenpox ☐   Measles ☐   Mumps ☐   Pneumonia ☐

Frequent colds or sore throat ☐   Ear infections ☐

_____

_____

_____

Additional Information _____

_____

_____

_____

_____

_____

_____

_____

_____

Medical History

Date _____

Child's Name _____ Blood Type _____

Doctor _____

Address _____ Telephone _____

Date of last physical exam _____

Birthmarks (Location) _____

Distinguishing marks, scars, etc. _____

Operations or Fractures (Dates) _____

Describe any speech impediments or handicaps _____

Name and Date of Last Serious Illness _____

Place of Record _____

Allergies (Specify) _____

Additional Pertinent Facts (Medications, Treatments, etc.) _____
_____
_____
_____
_____
_____
_____
_____

Dental Data

Date _____

Dentist _____

_____

Address _____

_____ Telephone _____

Visits to the Dentist _____ Dates _____

_____

_____

_____

Work Done _____ No. of Cavities _____

_____

_____

_____

_____

Braces _____ Missing Teeth _____ False Teeth _____

_____

Other Distinguishing Characteristics _____

_____

Other Pertinent Facts _____

_____

_____

Place of Record _____

A NEW DENTAL MICRODISC CHILD PROTECTION DEVICE

Dentists are now offering a tiny plastic identification disc that is bonded to the last upper right molar. It can be worn up to six years by the child.

The microdisc includes the wearer's name and address, telephone number and medical alert information, i.e. diabetic, epileptic, cardiac patient, allergies, special medications or other information.

This is a unique way to identify a child if he is lost, injured or unconscious. The disc can be popped off easily and read with proper instruments. All hospitals are being alerted to look for a dental microdisc in an injured or unconscious patient.

The microdisc, installation and office visit are not expensive. Ask your dentist.

Vital Documents

*God could not be everywhere,
and therefore he made mothers.*

Jewish Proverb

**Instructions
For Storage Pocket
See Page 79**

Contents

*Attach
Hair
Sample*

**Place Photo Inside
This Frame**

Date Photo Taken _____

Child's Full Name _____ *Nickname*_____

Age _____ *Weight*_____ *Height* _____ *Color: Eyes* _____ *Hair* _____

*Right or Left Handed?*_____ *Complexion* _____

*Glasses?*_____ *Contact Lenses?* _____

Personal Facts

Current Address

Street _____ Date _____

City _____ State _____

_____

Likes and Dislikes _____

_____

_____

Habits _____

_____

_____

Close Friends _____

_____

_____

_____

Special (Influential) People _____

_____

_____

_____

Favorite Clothing _____

_____

_____

Color _____

_____

Favorite Pastime _____

_____

Transportation To and From School _____

_____

After School Activities (Around the Neighborhood) _____

_____

_____

Other _____

_____

Medical History

Date _____

Child's Name _____ Blood Type _____

Doctor _____

Address _____ Telephone _____

_____

Date of last physical exam _____

Operations or Fractures (Dates) _____

_____

Allergies (Specify) _____

List All Medications, Treatments, etc. _____

_____

_____

Place of Record _____

Dental Data

Date _____

Dentist _____

Address _____ Telephone _____

_____

Dates Visit to the Dentist   Work Done

_____

_____

_____

_____

_____

Pertinent Facts _____

_____

_____

_____

_____

Place of Record _____

Vital Documents

*Children need models more
than they need critics.*
Joseph Joubert

**Instructions
For Storage Pocket
See Page 79**

Contents

_____
_____
_____
_____
_____
_____
_____
_____
_____

Attach Hair Sample

Place Photo Inside This Frame

Date Photo Taken _____

Child's Full Name _____ Nickname_____

Age _____ Weight_____ Height _____ Color: Eyes _____ Hair _____

Right or Left Handed? _____ Complexion _____

Glasses?_____ Contact Lenses? _____

Personal Facts

Current Address

Street _____ Date _____

City _____ State _____

_____

Likes and Dislikes _____

_____

_____

Habits _____

_____

_____

Close Friends _____

_____

_____

_____

Special (Influential) People _____

_____

_____

_____

Favorite Clothing _____

_____

_____

Color _____

_____

Favorite Pastime _____

_____

Transportation To and From School _____

_____

After School Activities (Around the Neighborhood) _____

_____

_____

_____

Other _____

_____

Medical History

Date _____

Child's Name _____

Blood Type _____

Doctor _____

Address _____ Telephone _____

_____

Date of last physical exam_____

Operations or Fractures (Dates) _____

_____

Allergies (Specify) _____

List All Medications, Treatments, etc. _____

_____

_____

Place of Record _____

_____

Dental Data

Date _____

Dentist _____

Address _____ Telephone _____

_____

Dates Visit to the Dentist   Work Done

_____

_____

_____

_____

_____

Pertinent Facts _____

_____

_____

_____

_____

Place of Record _____

_____

Vital Documents

Give a child a little love and
you get a great deal back.

John Ruskin

Instructions
For Storage Pocket
See Page 79

Contents

_____
_____
_____
_____
_____
_____
_____
_____
_____
_____

Attach
Hair
Sample

**Place Photo Inside
This Frame**

Date Photo Taken _____

Child's Full Name _____ *Nickname* _____

Age _____ *Weight* _____ *Height* _____ *Color: Eyes* _____ *Hair* _____

Right or Left Handed? _____ *Complexion* _____

Glasses? _____ *Contact Lenses?* _____

30

Personal Facts

Current Address

Street _____ Date _____

City _____ State _____

_____

Likes and Dislikes _____

_____

_____

Habits _____

_____

_____

Close Friends _____

_____

_____

Special (Influential) People _____

_____

_____

_____

Favorite Clothing _____

_____

_____

Color _____

_____

Favorite Pastime _____

_____

Transportation To and From School _____

_____

After School Activities (Around the Neighborhood) _____

_____

_____

Other _____

_____

Medical History

Date _____

Child's Name _____ Blood Type _____

Doctor _____

Address _____ Telephone _____

_____

Date of last physical exam _____

Operations or Fractures (Dates) _____

_____

Allergies (Specify) _____

List All Medications, Treatments, etc. _____

_____

_____

Place of Record _____

_____

Dental Data

Date _____

Dentist _____

Address _____ Telephone _____

Dates Visit to the Dentist   Work Done

_____

_____

_____

_____

_____

Pertinent Facts _____

_____

_____

_____

_____

Place of Record _____

_____

Vital Documents

The most important thing
a father can do for his children
is to love their mother.

The Rev. Theodore Hesburgh
President of Notre Dame University

Instructions
For Storage Pocket
See Page 79

Contents

_____
_____
_____
_____
_____
_____
_____
_____
_____
_____

*Attach
Hair
Sample*

**Place Photo Inside
This Frame**

Date Photo Taken _____

Child's Full Name _____ *Nickname*_____

Age _____ *Weight*_____ *Height* _____ *Color: Eyes* _____ *Hair* _____

*Right or Left Handed?*_____ *Complexion* _____

*Glasses?*_____ *Contact Lenses?* _____

Personal Facts

Current Address

Street _____ Date _____

City _____ State _____

_____

Likes and Dislikes _____

_____

_____

Habits _____

_____

_____

Close Friends _____

_____

_____

_____

Special (Influential) People _____

_____

_____

_____

Favorite Clothing _____

_____

_____

Color _____

_____

Favorite Pastime _____

_____

Transportation To and From School _____

_____

After School Activities (Around the Neighborhood) _____

_____

_____

Other _____

_____

Medical History

Date _____

Child's Name _____ Blood Type _____

Doctor _____

Address _____ Telephone _____

_____

Date of last physical exam _____

Operations or Fractures (Dates) _____

_____

Allergies (Specify) _____

List All Medications, Treatments, etc. _____

_____

_____

Place of Record _____

_____

Dental Data

Date _____

Dentist _____

Address _____ Telephone _____

_____

Dates Visit to the Dentist   Work Done

_____

_____

_____

_____

_____

Pertinent Facts _____

_____

_____

_____

_____

Place of Record _____

_____

Vital Documents

*If children grew up according
to early indications, we would
have nothing but geniuses.*

Johann Wolfgang von Goethe

**Instructions
For Storage Pocket
See Page 79**

Contents

*Attach
Hair
Sample*

**Place Photo Inside
This Frame**

Date Photo Taken _____

Child's Full Name _____ *Nickname*_____

Age _____ *Weight*_____ *Height* _____ *Color: Eyes* _____ *Hair* _____

*Right or Left Handed?*_____ *Complexion* _____

*Glasses?*_____ *Contact Lenses?*_____

Personal Facts

Current Address

Street _____ Date _____

City _____ State _____

Likes and Dislikes _____

_____

_____

Habits _____

_____

_____

Close Friends _____

_____

_____

Special (Influential) People _____

_____

_____

_____

Favorite Clothing _____

_____

_____

Color _____

_____

Favorite Pastime _____

_____

Transportation To and From School _____

_____

After School Activities (Around the Neighborhood) _____

_____

_____

Other _____

_____

Medical History

Date _____

Child's Name _____ Blood Type _____

Doctor _____

Address _____ Telephone _____

_____

Date of last physical exam _____

Operations or Fractures (Dates) _____

_____

Allergies (Specify) _____

List All Medications, Treatments, etc. _____

_____

_____

Place of Record _____

_____

Dental Data

Date _____

Dentist _____

Address _____ Telephone _____

_____

Dates Visit to the Dentist   Work Done

_____

_____

_____

_____

_____

Pertinent Facts _____

_____

_____

_____

_____

Place of Record _____

_____

Vital Documents

Train up a child in the way he
should go: and when he is old
he will not depart from it.

Proverbs 22:6

Instructions
For Storage Pocket
See Page 79

Contents

Attach Hair Sample

Place Photo Inside This Frame

Date Photo Taken _____

Child's Full Name _____ *Nickname* _____

Age _____ *Weight* _____ *Height* _____ *Color: Eyes* _____ *Hair* _____

Right or Left Handed? _____ *Complexion* _____

Glasses? _____ *Contact Lenses?* _____

Personal Facts

Current Address

Street _____ Date _____

City _____ State _____

Likes and Dislikes _____

_____

Habits _____

_____

Close Friends _____

_____

_____

Special (Influential) People _____

_____

_____

Favorite Clothing _____

_____

Color _____

Favorite Pastime _____

_____

Transportation To and From School _____

After School Activities (Around the Neighborhood) _____

_____

Other _____

_____

Medical History

Date _____

Child's Name _____

Blood Type _____

Doctor _____

Address _____ Telephone _____

_____

Date of last physical exam _____

Operations or Fractures (Dates) _____

_____

Allergies (Specify) _____

List All Medications, Treatments, etc. _____

_____

_____

Place of Record _____

_____

Dental Data

Date _____

Dentist _____

Address _____ Telephone _____

_____

Dates Visit to the Dentist   Work Done

_____

_____

_____

_____

_____

Pertinent Facts _____

_____

_____

_____

_____

Place of Record _____

_____

Vital Documents

Like father, like son: every
good tree maketh good fruit.
William Langlan

Instructions
For Storage Pocket
See Page 79

Contents

*Attach
Hair
Sample*

**Place Photo Inside
This Frame**

Date Photo Taken _____

Child's Full Name _____ *Nickname*_____

Age _____ *Weight*_____ *Height* _____ *Color: Eyes* _____ *Hair* _____

*Right or Left Handed?*_____ *Complexion* _____

*Glasses?*_____ *Contact Lenses?* _____

Personal Facts

Current Address

Street_____ Date _____

City_____ State _____

_____

Likes and Dislikes _____

_____

_____

Habits_____

_____

_____

Close Friends _____

_____

_____

_____

Special (Influential) People _____

_____

_____

_____

Favorite Clothing_____

_____

_____

Color _____

_____

Favorite Pastime _____

_____

Transportation To and From School_____

_____

After School Activities (Around the Neighborhood) _____

_____

_____

Other _____

_____

Medical History

Date _____

Child's Name _____ Blood Type _____

Doctor _____

Address _____ Telephone _____

Date of last physical exam _____

Operations or Fractures (Dates) _____

Allergies (Specify) _____

List All Medications, Treatments, etc. _____

_____

Place of Record _____

Dental Data

Date _____

Dentist _____

Address _____ Telephone _____

Dates Visit to the Dentist _____ Work Done

_____

_____

_____

_____

Pertinent Facts _____

_____

_____

_____

Place of Record _____

_____

Vital Documents

Even a child is known by his doings, whether his work be pure, and whether it be right.

Proverbs 20:11

Instructions For Storage Pocket See Page 79

Contents

_____

_____

_____

_____

_____

_____

_____

_____

_____

*Attach
Hair
Sample*

**Place Photo Inside
This Frame**

Date Photo Taken _____

Child's Full Name _____ *Nickname*_____

Age _____ *Weight*_____ *Height* _____ *Color: Eyes* _____ *Hair* _____

*Right or Left Handed?*_____*Complexion* _____

*Glasses?*_____*Contact Lenses?* _____

Personal Facts

Current Address

Street _____ Date _____

City _____ State _____

Likes and Dislikes _____

_____

Habits _____

_____

Close Friends _____

_____

_____

Special (Influential) People _____

_____

_____

Favorite Clothing _____

_____

Color _____

_____

Favorite Pastime _____

_____

Transportation To and From School _____

_____

After School Activities (Around the Neighborhood) _____

_____

Other _____

_____

Medical History

Date _____

Child's Name _____ Blood Type _____

Doctor _____

Address _____ Telephone _____

_____

Date of last physical exam _____

Operations or Fractures (Dates) _____

_____

Allergies (Specify) _____

List All Medications, Treatments, etc. _____

_____

_____

Place of Record _____

_____

Dental Data

Date _____

Dentist _____

Address _____ Telephone _____

Dates Visit to the Dentist   Work Done

_____

_____

_____

_____

_____

Pertinent Facts _____

_____

_____

_____

_____

Place of Record _____

_____

Vital Documents

It is a wise father that knows his own child.

William Shakespeare

**Instructions
For Storage Pocket
See Page 79**

Contents

Attach
Hair
Sample

Place Photo Inside
This Frame

Date Photo Taken _____

Child's Full Name _____ *Nickname*_____

Age _____ *Weight*_____ *Height* _____ *Color: Eyes* _____ *Hair* _____

*Right or Left Handed?*_____ *Complexion* _____

*Glasses?*_____ *Contact Lenses?*_____

Personal Facts

Current Address

Street _____ Date _____

City _____ State _____

_____

Likes and Dislikes _____

_____

_____

Habits _____

_____

_____

Close Friends _____

_____

_____

_____

Special (Influential) People _____

_____

_____

_____

Favorite Clothing _____

_____

_____

Color _____

_____

Favorite Pastime _____

_____

Transportation To and From School _____

_____

After School Activities (Around the Neighborhood) _____

_____

_____

Other _____

_____

Medical History

Date _____

Child's Name _____ Blood Type _____

Doctor _____

Address _____ Telephone _____

_____

Date of last physical exam _____

Operations or Fractures (Dates) _____

_____

Allergies (Specify) _____

List All Medications, Treatments, etc. _____

_____

_____

Place of Record _____

_____

Dental Data

Date _____

Dentist _____

Address _____ Telephone _____

Dates Visit to the Dentist   Work Done

_____

_____

_____

_____

_____

Pertinent Facts _____

_____

_____

_____

_____

Place of Record _____

_____

Vital Documents

*Suffer the little children to come
unto me, and forbid them not:
for of such is the kingdom of God.*

Mark 10:14

**Instructions
For Storage Pocket
See Page 79**

Contents

Attach Hair Sample

Place Photo Inside This Frame

Date Photo Taken _____

Child's Full Name _____ *Nickname*_____

Age _____ *Weight*_____ *Height* _____ *Color: Eyes* _____ *Hair* _____

*Right or Left Handed?*_____*Complexion* _____

*Glasses?*_____*Contact Lenses?*_____

Personal Facts

Current Address

Street _____ Date _____

City _____ State _____

_____

Likes and Dislikes _____

_____

_____

Habits _____

_____

_____

Close Friends _____

_____

_____

_____

Special (Influential) People _____

_____

_____

_____

Favorite Clothing _____

_____

_____

Color _____

_____

Favorite Pastime _____

_____

Transportation To and From School _____

_____

After School Activities (Around the Neighborhood) _____

_____

_____

Other _____

_____

Medical History

Date _____

Child's Name _____ Blood Type _____

Doctor _____

Address _____ Telephone _____

_____

Date of last physical exam _____

Operations or Fractures (Dates) _____

_____

Allergies (Specify) _____

List All Medications, Treatments, etc. _____

_____

_____

Place of Record _____

_____

Dental Data

Date _____

Dentist _____

Address _____ Telephone _____

_____

Dates Visit to the Dentist   Work Done

_____

_____

_____

_____

_____

Pertinent Facts _____

_____

_____

_____

_____

Place of Record _____

_____

Vital Documents

*One of the best things in the
world to be is a boy; it requires
no experience, but needs some
practice to be a good one.*
Charles Dudley Warner

**Instructions
For Storage Pocket
See Page 79**

Contents

Attach
Hair
Sample

Place Photo Inside
This Frame

Date Photo Taken _____

Child's Full Name _____ *Nickname*_____

Age _____ *Weight* _____ *Height* _____ *Color: Eyes* _____ *Hair* _____

*Right or Left Handed?*_____ *Complexion* _____

*Glasses?*_____ *Contact Lenses?*_____

Personal Facts

Current Address

Street _____ Date _____

City _____ State _____

_____

Likes and Dislikes _____

_____

_____

Habits _____

_____

_____

Close Friends _____

_____

_____

_____

Special (Influential) People _____

_____

_____

_____

Favorite Clothing _____

_____

_____

Color _____

_____

Favorite Pastime _____

_____

Transportation To and From School _____

_____

After School Activities (Around the Neighborhood) _____

_____

_____

Other _____

_____

Medical History

Date _____

Child's Name _____ Blood Type _____

Doctor _____

Address _____ Telephone _____

_____

Date of last physical exam _____

Operations or Fractures (Dates) _____

_____

Allergies (Specify) _____

List All Medications, Treatments, etc. _____

_____

_____

Place of Record _____

_____

Dental Data

Date _____

Dentist _____

Address _____ Telephone _____

_____

Dates Visit to the Dentist   Work Done

_____

_____

_____

_____

_____

Pertinent Facts _____

_____

_____

_____

Place of Record _____

_____

Contents

_____
_____
_____
_____
_____
_____
_____
_____
_____

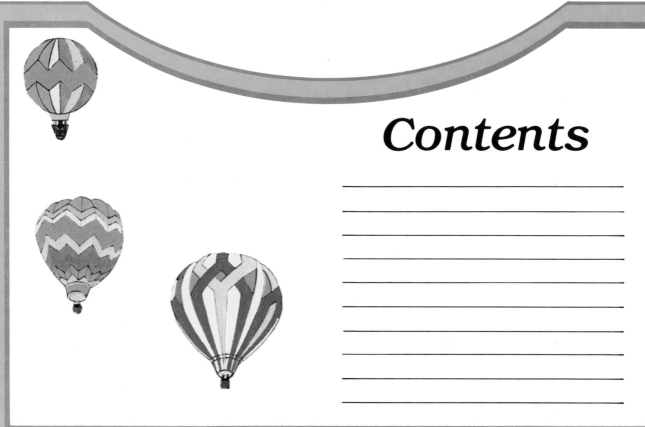

Contents

_____
_____
_____
_____
_____
_____
_____
_____
_____

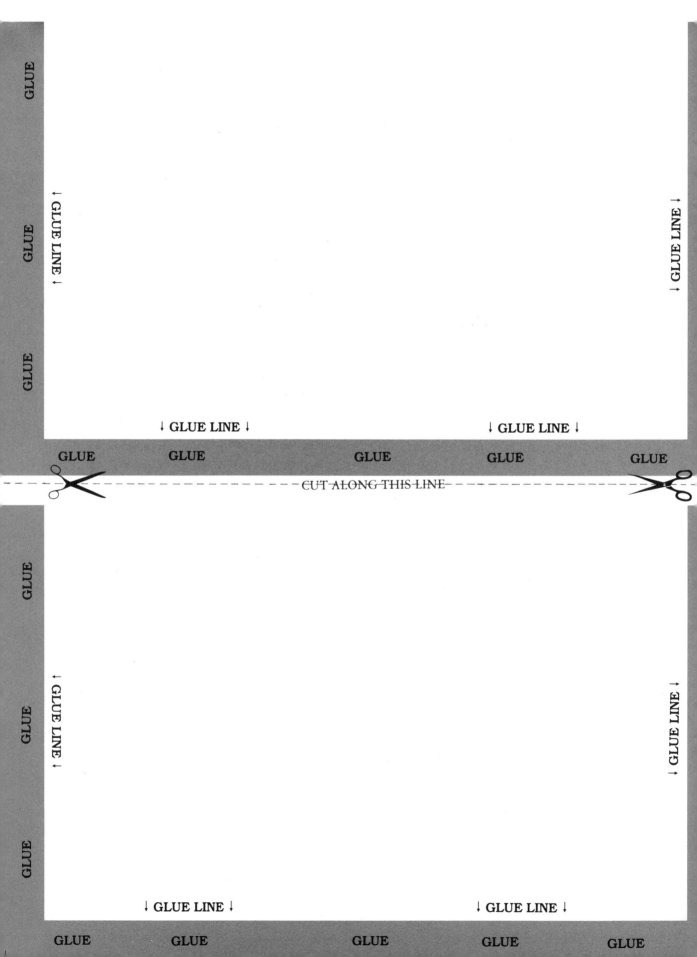

GLUE

GLUE

↑ GLUE LINE ↓

↓ GLUE LINE ↑

GLUE

↓ GLUE LINE ↓

↓ GLUE LINE ↓

GLUE GLUE GLUE GLUE GLUE

CUT ALONG THIS LINE

GLUE

GLUE

↑ GLUE LINE ↓

↓ GLUE LINE ↑

GLUE

↓ GLUE LINE ↓

↓ GLUE LINE ↓

GLUE GLUE GLUE GLUE GLUE

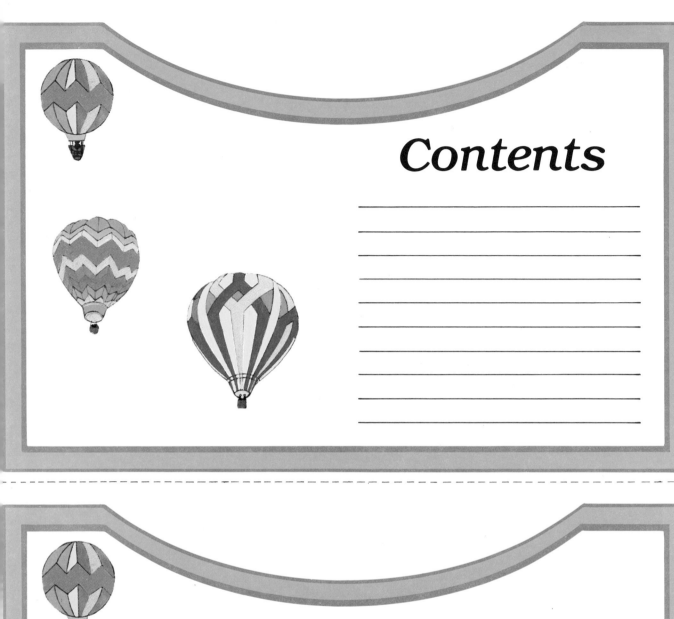

Contents

_____
_____
_____
_____
_____
_____
_____
_____
_____
_____

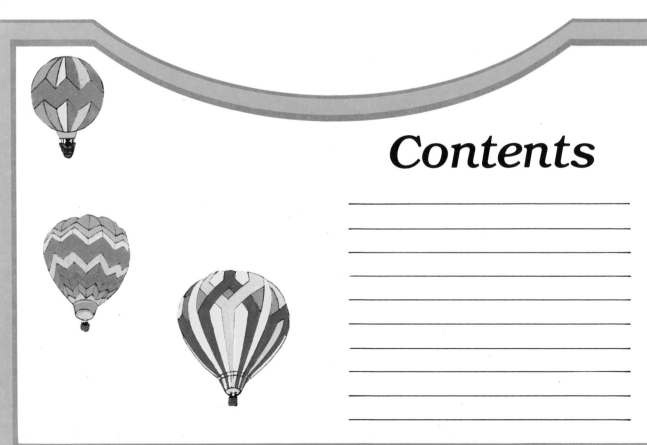

Contents

_____
_____
_____
_____
_____
_____
_____
_____
_____
_____

Contents

_____
_____
_____
_____
_____
_____
_____
_____
_____

Contents

_____
_____
_____
_____
_____
_____
_____
_____
_____

GLUE

GLUE

GLUE

↓ GLUE LINE ↓

GLUE LINE

↓ GLUE LINE ↓

↓ GLUE LINE ↓

GLUE GLUE GLUE GLUE GLUE

CUT ALONG THIS LINE

GLUE

GLUE

GLUE

↓ GLUE LINE ↓

GLUE LINE

↓ GLUE LINE ↓

↓ GLUE LINE ↓

GLUE GLUE GLUE GLUE GLUE

Contents

_____
_____
_____
_____
_____
_____
_____
_____
_____

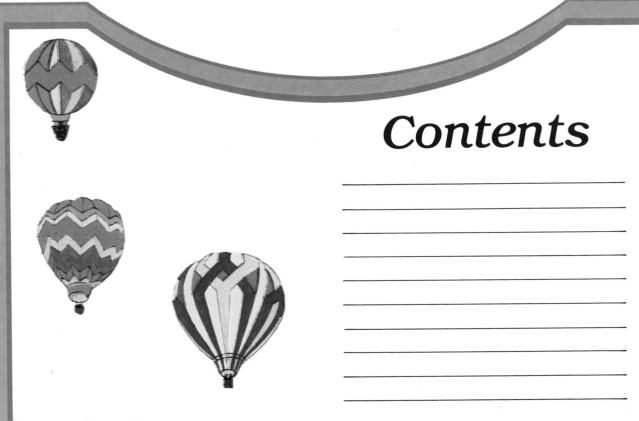

Contents

_____
_____
_____
_____
_____
_____
_____

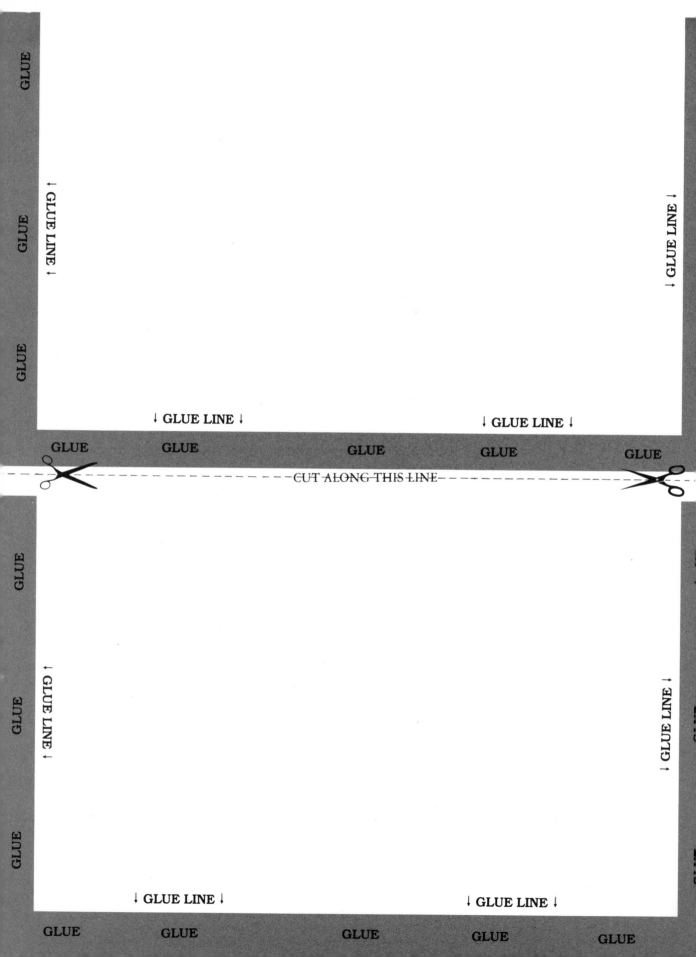

Contents

_____
_____
_____
_____
_____
_____
_____
_____

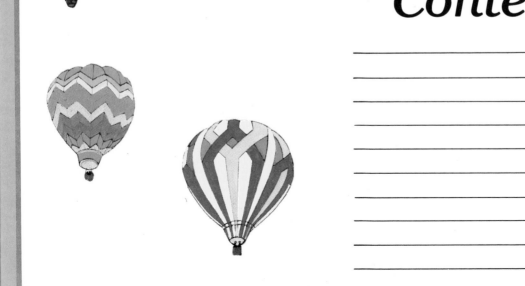

Contents

_____
_____
_____
_____
_____
_____
_____
_____

Contents

_____
_____
_____
_____
_____
_____
_____
_____
_____
_____

Contents

_____
_____
_____
_____
_____
_____
_____
_____
_____

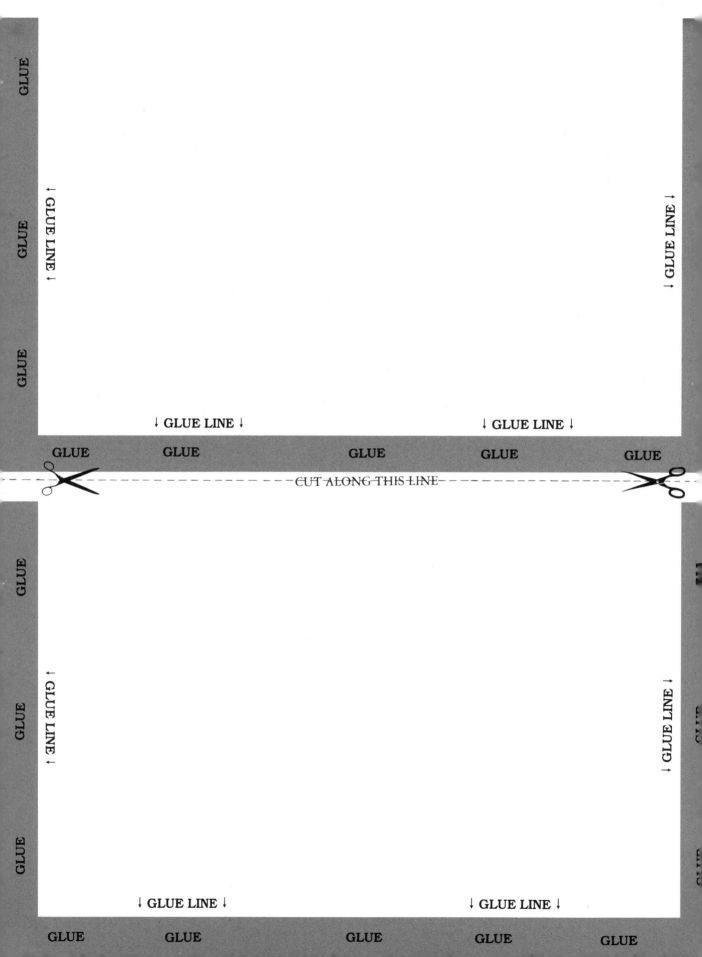

Fingerprint Card

Date _____

Child's Full Name _____
LAST   FIRST   MIDDLE

Residence_____
STREET   CITY   STATE

Height _____ Weight _____ Sex _____

Race _____ Color: Eyes _____ Hair _____

Hair Texture: Straight ☐   Wavy ☐   Curly ☐

Skin Complexion: White ☐   Dark Brown ☐   Light Brown ☐   Olive ☐

Other ☐

Right or Left Handed? _____ Visible Scars or Marks? _____

Date of Birth _____ Place of Birth _____

1. RIGHT THUMB	2. RIGHT INDEX	3. RIGHT MIDDLE	4. RIGHT RING	5. RIGHT LITTLE

6. LEFT THUMB	7. LEFT INDEX	8. LEFT MIDDLE	9. LEFT RING	10. LEFT LITTLE

LEFT FOUR FINGERS TAKEN SIMULTANEOUSLY	L. THUMB	R. THUMB	RIGHT FOUR FINGERS TAKEN SIMULTANEOUSLY

Fingerprinting is for professionals. If you do not already have a copy of your child's fingerprints, contact your local police department. They can fingerprint your child and give you the card for safekeeping. It will take only five minutes.

'Palm 'Prints

left palm

right palm